# KINDERGA

# Bible Games

## Written by Mary J. Davis
## Illustrated by Carol Tiernon
## Cover Illustrated by Judy Hierstein

### Dedication

With love to my husband and children.
With thanks to my parents and in-laws.
With wonderful memories of my siblings, all 10 of you.

All rights reserved—Printed in the U.S.A.
Copyright © 1999 Shining Star Publications
A Division of Frank Schaffer Publications, Inc.
23740 Hawthorne Blvd., Torrance, CA 90505

**Notice!** Pages may be reproduced for home or classroom use only, not for commercial resale. No part of this publication may be reproduced for storage in a retrieval system, or transmitted in any form or by any means—electronic, mechanical, recording, etc.—without the prior written permission of the publisher. Reproduction of these materials for an entire school or school system is strictly prohibited.

Unless otherwise indicated, the New International Version of the Bible was used in preparing the activities in this book. Scripture taken from the HOLY BIBLE, NEW INTERNATIONAL VERSION. Copyright © 1973, 1978, 1984 International Bible Society. Used by permission of Zondervan Bible Publishers.

# Table of Contents

# To Teachers and Parents

**W**hat a fantastic way to help kindergarteners learn all about God and His love for us and develop some valuable skills at the same time!

*Bible Games* has been created to provide opportunities for children of kindergarten age to develop such valuable skills as following directions, visual discrimination, counting, sequencing, memorization, cutting, pasting, coloring, working with others, and many more, as they play stimulating games based on Christian values and principles.

The book is divided into these five sections: Action Games (Group); Songs, Chants, Action Rhymes, and Stories (Group); Quiet and Paper Games (Group); Games for Small Groups/Pairs; and Games for Individuals. This allows you to choose the kind of game or activity that will best suit your group.

Each game is based on God and His love for us, and many feature Bible references. Refer to these when the children play the games to help them better understand the underlying theme of the game and God's love for us and some important Christian values.

Assume an active role as you guide the children in playing the games presented in this book. You will have a wonderful time watching the children have great fun as their love for God deepens and they practice and improve a wonderful variety of skills all kindergarten children need!

# Find Jesus' Helpers

### Mark 3:13–19

This game will help the children learn all about Jesus' special helpers.

Copy, cut out, and hide the patterns of the 12 disciples below and on pages 5–6 around the room. Encourage the children to find Jesus' helpers. Repeat their names often so the children will begin to recognize them. You may also want to count the figures to give the children a concrete idea that Jesus had 12 special helpers called disciples. You can use these patterns for any stories involving the disciples.

1

Peter

2

Andrew

3

James

© Shining Star Publications

SS48842

# Find Jesus' Helpers

continued

4 Simon

5 Philip

6 James

7 Matthew

© Shining Star Publications

SS48842

# Find Jesus' Helpers

continued

8 John

9 Thaddaeus

10 Thomas

11 Bartholomew

12 Judas

© Shining Star Publications

6

SS48842

# Jesus Loves Us Toss

Matthew 19:13–15

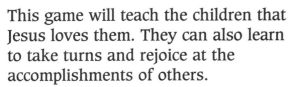

This game will teach the children that Jesus loves them. They can also learn to take turns and rejoice at the accomplishments of others.

Divide the children into groups. Give each group a copy of the patterns below and on page 8. The strips on page 8 need to be cut out and taped so that each forms a ring. Cut out the figure of Jesus and fold on the center dotted line. Fold on the bottom dotted lines, tape together, and stand Jesus up. (You may want to make all patterns sturdier by laminating them or by gluing them to construction paper. You may also want to enlarge the Jesus pattern, just make sure the rings can be tossed over Him easily.)

Read the children Matthew 19:13–15 and tell the story many times while the children try to throw the rings around Jesus from a designated spot.

Fold and tape.

Fold and tape.

# Jesus Loves Us Toss

### continued

**Directions:**
Tape tab A to tab B. Then tape tab C to tab D.

© Shining Star Publications

SS48842

# Bowl Over the Philistines

**1 Samuel 17**

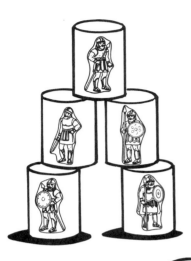

This game is perfect to use with the story of David and Goliath or any story involving Philistines. The children will be excited as they "bowl over" the bad guys!

Make one game for the whole class to play together. You will need five juice cans and a beanbag or plastic ball. Cut out the five Philistine patterns below and on page 10 and glue one to each can. Set up the cans in a pyramid formation. Children throw the beanbag or roll the ball to knock over the Philistines.

For more fun, make two copies of the patterns below and on page 10 and use 10 juice cans to make a complete bowling set of 10.

© Shining Star Publications

SS48842

# Bowl Over the Philistines

### continued

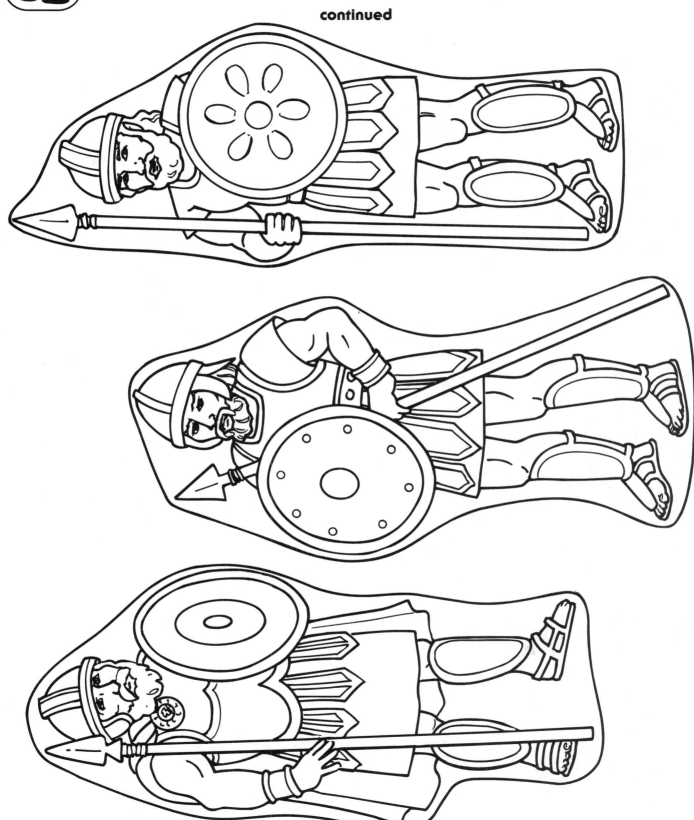

# Put Him in the Tree

**Luke 19:1–10**

Children can learn how Jesus forgave sinners with this story and game.

Make enough copies of the Zacchaeus patterns below so that each child gets one. Enlarge and cut out the tree on page 12. Tape the tree to a wall at a height the children can easily reach. Cut out the Zacchaeus patterns and put a loop of tape on the back of each one. Give each child one.

If the children do not want to be blindfolded, cover the lenses of a pair of sunglasses with paper or foil. Put the "blinder" glasses on one child. Turn the child around in a circle once or twice, then point him or her toward the tree. The child should attempt to put Zacchaeus on a branch in the tree.

This game can be an "everybody wins" game by allowing any area inside the tree to be the winning area.

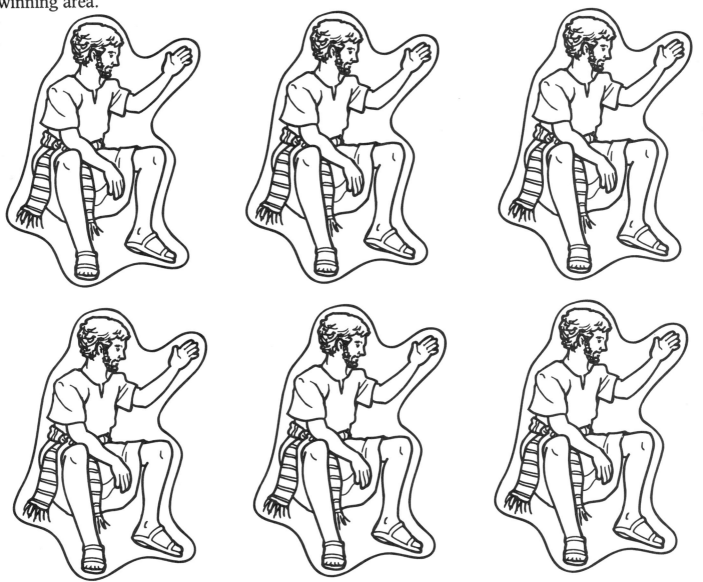

© Shining Star Publications

SS48842

# Put Him in the Tree

### continued

© Shining Star Publications

SS48842

# Who's Calling?

## 1 Samuel 3:1–9

"Samuel, Samuel"

This game is perfect to use to help the children learn how God called to Samuel.

To play, choose one child to be Samuel. Samuel covers his eyes. Someone else in the room calls, "Samuel, Samuel." Then Samuel uncovers his eyes and tries to guess who called his name. Repeat the game, giving all children a chance to be Samuel and letting all children have a turn to call Samuel's name.

# Run Across the Sea

## Exodus 14

Before and after this game, talk about how the Israelites crossed the Red Sea on dry ground and how Moses raised his hand over the sea to separate it and again to make the sea flow over the Egyptians.

This can be an outside or inside game. Choose one child to be Moses. All other children will line up against one wall or at a designated spot outside. This is the starting place. Mark off another spot opposite the starting place. Children will be "safe" at either spot.

When Moses raises his or her hand, children must run toward the other side of the "sea." When Moses lowers his hand quickly and shouts "Stop," any children in the middle of the sea must stop. Moses may choose one of these children to replace him.

# Pillars of Salt

### Genesis 19:15–26

"It"

"Lot"

"Pillar of salt"

The story of Lot's wife turning into a pillar of salt is fascinating for most children. This tag game gives them the perfect opportunity to act out the story.

This game can be played indoors or outside. Choose one child to be "It" and one to be Lot. When a child is tagged by "It," he or she becomes a pillar of salt. Then Lot can run to tag the "pillars of salt" and set them free. Change "It" and Lot several times throughout the game.

# Mighty Wind Race

### Exodus 14; Matthew 8:23–27

This game is great to use when discussing the stories of God drying up the sea for the Israelites to cross and Jesus calming the storm.

Provide each of at least six children with a Ping-Pong ball. Each of these six children begins at a starting point on his or her knees. On "Go," the children blow their Ping-Pong balls a specified distance to a winning point. Repeat until all children have raced at least once.

© Shining Star Publications

SS48842

# I Am Growing

## Luke 2; 1 Samuel 1

A safe obstacle course children can go through, inside and outside, is perfect to use to help teach a variety of Bible stories. Stories to accompany this game include Jesus or Samuel as children (Luke 2, 1 Samuel 1, respectively).

**Some suggestions of items to include in the obstacle course are as follows:**

- a beanbag chair to jump over
- a mini trampoline to jump on
- a v-shaped tent to crawl through (a blanket over a rope)
- a block maze to walk through without stepping on the blocks
- a trash can barricade to go around
- papers taped to the ground or floor that must be avoided
- a lion's den (a stuffed toy enclosed in a fence of blocks) to tiptoe through
- streamers hanging from the ceiling to break through

© Shining Star Publications

SS48842

# Stomp Out That Sin

This game is great to use with any story. It helps the children focus on helping others to keep from sinning.

Tie a length of crepe paper loosely to each child's ankle, leaving around two or three feet of paper touching the floor. On "Go," children stomp out each other's sin by trying to tear each other's crepe paper off, using only their feet. The game continues until everyone's sin has been stomped out.

# Build the Tabernacle

The purpose of this game is teamwork and to help the children understand how much work it was for the Israelites to set up the tabernacle each time they made a stop on their way to the Promised Land. Stories to use with this game include traveling in the wilderness (Exodus and Deuteronomy) or building the tabernacle (Exodus 26).

Divide children into at least two teams. Place a large sheet of newsprint, a table covering, or an old bed sheet on the floor for each team. Give the team members 8 1/2" x 11" or larger sheets of scrap paper. Let the children work for a certain amount of time, trying to cover the entire space with the scrap paper. At the end of the allotted time, judge whose tabernacle looks the most complete.

# Feeding Elijah

## 1 Kings 17:1–6

Children will better understand how God takes care of His people with this game.

Make one copy of the patterns below. Glue Elijah to a paper bag, an oatmeal container, or a tall cracker box. Cut out the raven and glue it to a spring clothespin. Create "food" using anything you have on hand, such as wadded up paper or tissue, cotton balls, cotton swabs, or crayons.

Have the children stand on chairs and try to drop the "food" to feed Elijah into the container by releasing it from the clothespin raven.

This can be an "everyone wins" game by making sure the distance above the container is short. It can be a challenging game by having the children toss the raven into the container from a distance.

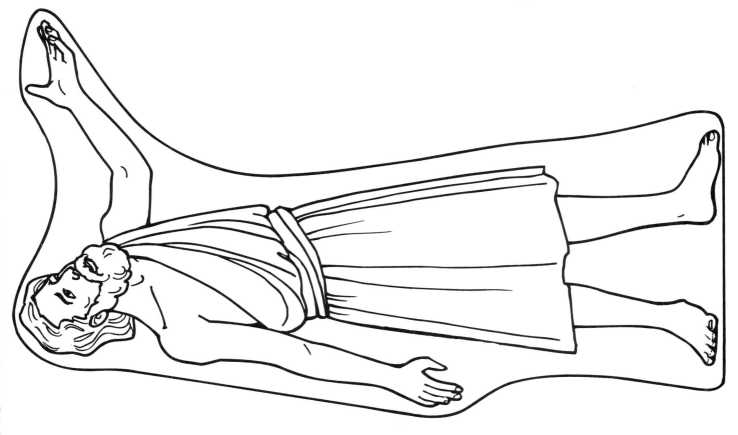

© Shining Star Publications

SS48842

# Adam's Friends

### Genesis 1:20–25, Genesis 6–9

Use this game inside or outside. It can be used for the stories of Creation, Noah's Ark, or any other animal stories.

Make a copy of the patterns below and on page 19. Glue each animal to an index card. Then place the cards upside down.

Have a child pick a card and not show it to anyone. The child can then act like that animal, and the others can guess which animal he or she is.

# Adam's Friends

continued

© Shining Star Publications

SS48842

# Naaman's Bath

## 2 Kings 5:1–15

Explain to the children that Naaman had to do exactly as Elisha instructed him, or he would not have been healed of his leprosy. Then let them play the game below in which they must do exactly as "Elisha" says.

One child is Elisha; the rest are Naaman. Elisha stands with his back to the others. Each child takes turns calling out, "Elisha, how many times must I dip in the Jordan?" Elisha says a number up to 7. Elisha may also say, "Start over." The children take the number of steps Elisha says. When a child reaches Elisha, he or she becomes Elisha.

© Shining Star Publications

SS48842

# Follow Jesus

This game is fun to use with any Christian concept. Be sure to stress that as Christians, we need to follow the path to God. (This can be played with more than one team, or it can be played just for fun.)

In a large open space, provide one roll of bathroom tissue for each group of five children. Each group stands in a line, one child behind the other. The first child steps on the end of the tissue and gives the roll a push with his or her other foot. This creates a path with the tissue. Then this child moves to the back of the line and the next child stands where the roll stopped, puts his or her foot on the tissue, and gives the roll a push with his or her other foot.

The game continues until the roll of tissue is completely unrolled. As the children are playing, discuss ways they can follow in Jesus' footsteps to reach God in heaven.

# Find Baby Moses

### Exodus 2:1–10

Moses played such an important role in the history of the Israelites. Let the children play the game below to learn all about him.

Cut out the pattern of baby Moses below. Trace around the oval shape several times on brown construction paper or on a brown paper bag. Cut out these shapes. Glue the picture of Moses on the back of one of the shapes. Hide the baskets and let the children search for Moses. The child who finds the correct basket may retell the story of baby Moses to the class.

© Shining Star Publications

SS48842

# Bible Carnival Games

The games below are perfect to use for a Sunday school rally, a vacation Bible school celebration, or any event that calls for carnival-type games. Be sure to discuss the Bible passages listed with the children.

### Goliath Must Fall
(1 Samuel 17)

Children throw beanbags at plastic bowling pins. Faces may be drawn on the pins to look like Goliath. Set the pins up in a line and let the children try to knock down one pin.

### Fishy Fun
Children can try to find plastic fish in blue gelatin using their hands to feel while blindfolded.

### Guess the Great Catch
(Luke 5:1–11)

Children can guess how many fish crackers are in a pond (bowl).

### Coin in Fish's Mouth
(Matthew 17:24–27)

Children drop a coin into a jar of water that has a small glass inside. If the coin goes into the small glass, the child wins.

### Jonah Soaker
(Jonah 1–3)

Children throw wet sponges into a fish's mouth (trash can).

### Bee-attitudes
Make simple bees from paper and fan out the back. Glue each to a spring clothespin. Clip the clothespins to a thin clothesline that is at least 10 feet long and at a height children can easily reach. Children can blow on a bee until it gets to the other end of the line. This can be a relay or a race.

# Magnificent Miracles

### Matthew 14:13–21; 20:29–34; John 2:1–11

This game is perfect to use with any of the miracle stories found throughout the Bible.

Provide the items mentioned below for the children. Help the children pretend to be in need of a miracle by doing the actions described. Discuss some of the miracles Jesus performed.

- Try to walk with both feet in a paper bag.

- Try to walk with both legs tied together with a strip of bathroom tissue.

- Try to pick up a paper clip with a large glove on.

- Try to unwrap a wrapped piece of candy while wearing two large gloves.

I'th airy ard oo awk.

- Try to throw a ball into a bucket with eyes closed.

- Help each other through a safe obstacle course.

- Try to speak while holding tongue.

- Four or more children can carefully try to lift one child lying on a blanket.

- Take turns pulling each other around on a blanket (helping a lame friend).

- Mouth words to the children without making a sound. The children can try to understand what you are saying.

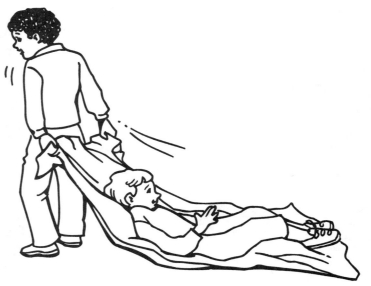

# Prison Wrap-up

Use this game with stories describing a Bible character who was in jail or prison (Paul, Peter, Joseph, John the Baptist, etc.).

Have the children sit in a circle. Use a roll of bathroom tissue. As you tell the Bible story, wrap a roll of bathroom tissue around the circle of children, in and out. At the end of the story, tell the children to "break out."

# A Hungry Lion

### Daniel 6

Daniel loved God with all his heart. Let the children learn all about this brave young man by playing the game below.

Have the children sit in a circle. One child is a lion. The lion goes around the circle and taps each child on the shoulder, saying "lion." The lion touches one lion and says "hungry." When the child says "hungry," both children crawl on their knees around the circle and race back to the same spot. Children must go in the OPPOSITE direction of each other. The first one back gets to sit down. The other one is the lion.

# Follow the Leader

This game helps the children learn that we can follow Jesus no matter where we are.

Lead the children in several actions, such as hopping, skipping, running, waving, smiling, etc. Stress to the children that they are "following" what you tell them to do. Tell them that we can follow Jesus in all that we do. Have them come up with ways they can follow Jesus.

# Sing to God

The songs below are fun for the children to sing and fit any Bible story.

### Follow Him!

(Tune: "The Farmer in the Dell")

_____ (name of Bible character) followed God.

_____ followed God.

Although sometimes it was hard to do,

_____ followed God.

I can follow God.

I can follow God.

Although sometimes it's hard to do,

I can follow God.

### Let's Learn!

(Tune: "Here We Go 'Round the Mulberry Bush")

We learn about _____ (this can be a person, place, event) in God's Word,

In God's Word, in God's Word.

We learn about _____ in God's Word.

What a wonderful Book it is!

### The Greatest Commandments!

After the children learn the song below about loving God, have them march around the room singing. The children can take turns being the leader.

(Tune: "Here We Go 'Round the Mulberry Bush")

Love the Lord God with all your heart,

With all your soul, and with all your mind.

And love your neighbor as yourself.

These are the greatest commandments.

# Don't Fall Overboard

**Matthew 8:23–27**

This song is a great way for children to learn the story of Jesus calming the storm. Sing the verses below to the tune of "London Bridge." Have the children get in a circle. Have two adults hold their arms out, hands touching, to form a cradle in which to catch the children. When you come to the phrase, "Don't fall overboard," enclose a child in the cradle and rock him or her as though he or she would fall into the water.

The big old storm rocked the boat,
Rocked the boat, rocked the boat.
The big old storm rocked the boat.
Don't fall overboard.

Jesus' friends were all afraid,
All afraid, all afraid.
Jesus' friends were all afraid.
Don't fall overboard.

Jesus told the storm to stop,
Storm to stop, storm to stop.
Jesus told the storm to stop.
Don't fall overboard.

© Shining Star Publications

SS48842

# Jump Rope Chants

These chants are fun to use when the children jump rope. They can also be sung as marching songs, with the children holding hands and going in a circle faster and faster. Or, let the children sing them as they wave streamers made from paper towel tubes and crepe paper.

### Praise Him
Praise Him, Praise Him.
1, 2, 3, 4
Praise Him, Praise Him.
Forevermore.

### God Made . . .
God made the earth,
And God made the sea.
God made all living things.
He even made me.

### Love
I love Mom.
I love Dad.
I love Jesus.
I love God.
(Children can add their own one-word endings to "I love . . .")

# Action Time!

Let the children act out the poem below. Remind them that as they grow physically, they need to remember to grow spiritually in God's love.

## Growing

I am growing
Oh, so tall.
The sky, sun, stars—
I can reach them all.
*(Stretch up.)*

I am growing.
Look at me!
I can reach
*(Point to self.)*
As high as the trees.
*(Stretch up.)*

I am growing
Every day.
I can run
And jump and play.
*(Jump up and down.)*

I am growing—
Watch and see.
I am very special
The way God made me.
*(Hug self.)*

© Shining Star Publications

SS48842

# A Seven-Day March

### Joshua 6:1–21

This is a great wiggle activity and is perfect to use after the children have heard the story of the walls of Jericho. Have the children march around in a circle, chanting, with nothing in the middle of the circle. At the end, all the children can fall into the middle of the circle.

**Chant:**

March around Jericho,

March around Jericho,

March around Jericho—

This is day 1.

*(Repeat chant up through "day 6." For day 7, have the children say the verse below.)*

Sound the trumpets;

Sound the trumpets;

Sound the trumpets;

On day 7, the walls fell DOWN!

# Commandment Chant

### Exodus 20

This game is great to help the children learn about obeying God's commands.

Tell the children to shout "I will" if you say a commandment that God wants them to do. Tell the children to shout "I will not" if you say a commandment that God doesn't want them to do. Let the children add any to the lists they want.

**I will not . . .**

lie

steal

worship other gods

want what others have

hurt someone

take what isn't mine

use God's name in the wrong way

make an idol

**I will . . .**

worship only God

obey my parents

tell the truth

remember the Sabbath

honor my parents

love others

# Tell a Bible Story

Have the children sit with you in a circle and pat their legs to make a noise like someone walking. Then tell a Bible story of your choice in rhythm. An example is below, but you may substitute any Bible story.

We're traveling through the wilderness,       *(Pat legs.)*
Following God's cloud.
It's starting to get dark. Let's hurry.      *(Pat legs faster.)*
Oh! Now we are very tired.      *(Pat legs slower.)*
Let's stop and rest for the night.      *(Stop patting.)*

Now it's morning. Everybody up.
We have lots of ground to cover.
Let's get going.      *(Begin to pat legs.)*

We can keep up with all those before us.
We just have to go a little bit faster.      *(Pat legs faster.)*
Ah, now we are keeping up.

Oh! Am I ever hungry! Is it lunchtime yet?
My legs are getting tired. Daddy, are we there yet?
Oh, good! It's time to stop for lunch.      *(Stop patting.)*

*(Finish the story in whatever direction you wish to take it.*
*This can be a wiggle activity, or you can tell an entire story.)*

# God Created Me

**Genesis 1:26–27**

The song below is fun for children to sing to learn all about the wonderful things God gave each of us when He created us.

(Tune: "Row, Row, Row Your Boat")

God created me.

God created me.

He gave me eyes to see.                    (*Blink eyes.*)

God created me.

For more verses, try substituting the lines below for line 3.

| | |
|---|---|
| He gave me ears to hear. | (*Cup hands to ears.*) |
| He gave me a mouth to speak. | (*Point to mouth.*) |
| He gave me arms to hug. | (*Hug a neighbor.*) |
| He gave me hands to wave. | (*Wave.*) |
| He gave me feet to walk. | (*Walk in place.*) |
| He gave me a heart to love. | (*Put hand on heart.*) |
| He gave me a mind to think. | (*Tap side of head with finger.*) |
| He gave me a nose to smell. | (*Wiggle nose with hand.*) |

# God's Church

This song helps the children better understand that the word *church* has several important meanings for Christians.

(Tune: "Jesus Loves Me")

| | |
|---|---|
| The church is not just a building | (*Make an upside down v with hands.*) |
| Made of brick or wood or stone. | (*Make a fist for stones.*) |
| The church is God's chosen people, | (*Point to self.*) |
| Worshipping together as one. | (*Hold hands.*) |
| We are the church. | (*Hold hands and raise them up.*) |
| We are the church. | |
| We are the church, | |
| Worshipping together as one. | |

# God vs. Baal

## 1 Kings 18:16–39

This action song provides a fun way for the children to learn all about Elijah and the prophets.

(Tune: "Hokey Pokey")
| | |
|---|---|
| The prophets shouted loud. | *(Cup hands to mouth.)* |
| The prophets screamed real loud. | *(Cup hands to mouth.)* |
| But no one answered their silly pleas. | *(Shake head "no.")* |
| They did a silly dance, | *(Dance.)* |
| And they turned themselves around. | *(Turn around.)* |
| What a silly bunch they were! | *(Shake index finger.)* |

## Chorus:

| | |
|---|---|
| Worship o-nly God. | *(Point to God.)* |
| Worship o-nly God. | |
| Worship o-nly God. | |
| That's what it's all about. | |

| | |
|---|---|
| They shook their hands to their gods. | *(Wiggle hands.)* |
| They shook their feet to their gods. | *(Wiggle feet.)* |
| But those false gods still did not help. | *(Shake head "no.")* |
| They did a silly dance, | *(Dance.)* |
| And they turned themselves around. | *(Turn around.)* |
| What a silly bunch they were! | *(Shake index finger.)* |

## Chorus

| | |
|---|---|
| They stood really tall. | *(Stretch tall.)* |
| They then bowed right down. | *(Stoop down.)* |
| They cried out to their gods again and again. | *(Cup hands to mouth.)* |
| They did a silly dance, | *(Dance.)* |
| And they turned themselves around. | *(Turn around.)* |
| What a silly bunch they were! | *(Shake index finger.)* |

## Chorus

| | |
|---|---|
| Then Elijah called out to his God. | *(Lift head up.)* |
| And on the first try, | *(Make a #1.)* |
| God did a great thing and sent a great big fire. | *(Form large circle with arms.)* |
| God burned up the offering, | *(Wiggle fingers as flames.)* |
| Altar and all. | |
| What a great God is He! | *(Point to God.)* |

## Chorus

# A Special New Life

This action story is perfect to use with any Creation or Resurrection theme.

Cut a piece of newsprint large enough to go around a child with his or her arms at his or her side, and loose enough to allow the child to crouch down inside. Tape closed. Make one of these "cocoons" for each child. Then do the action story below.

Little cocoon, little cocoon,　　　　　　(Crouch down.)
God made me a little cocoon.
I'm all wrapped up here inside.　　　　(Crouch lower.)
Some folks think I may have died.

But I am changing every day.　　　　　(Begin to stand.)
Soon I'll begin to break away.　　　　　(Stand up tall.)
A beautiful butterfly I will be.　　　　　(Break out.)
God has given new life to me.　　　　　(Flap arms.)

# Riding on a Donkey

Use this song as a wiggle activity or to review any donkey or traveling story.

(Tune: "The Wheels on the Bus")

The legs on the donkey go up and down,     *(Stoop down and back up.)*
Up and down, up and down.
The legs on the donkey go up and down,
All through the day.

The person on the donkey goes bounce,     *(Bounce as if on donkey.)*
    bounce, bounce,
Bounce, bounce, bounce; bounce,
    bounce, bounce.
The person on the donkey goes bounce,
    bounce, bounce,
All through the day.

The donkey's owner says, "Very good job,     *(Pat self on shoulder.)*
Very good job, very good job."
The donkey's owner says, "Very good job,"
All through the day.

God says to the donkey, "I'm proud of you,     *(Point to self and then away.)*
Proud of you, proud of you."
God says to the donkey, "I'm proud of you,"
All through the day.

© Shining Star Publications

SS48842

# Super Wise Men

**Matthew 2:1–12**

This song helps remind children of the great light the wise men followed to find baby Jesus.

(Tune: "Twinkle, Twinkle, Little Star")

Twinkle, twinkle, brightest star,          (*Put hands in air, wiggle fingers.*)
Help the wise men travel far.              (*Pretend to ride a camel.*)

Up above the world so high,               (*Stretch arms high.*)
As a guide light in the sky.              (*Put hands together to form
                                            a star.*)

Help us find this child of God,           (*Make cradle with arms.*)
So we can shower Him with love.           (*Cross arms and hold to chest.*)

# The Early Church

### Acts 5:1–11

This song will help the children learn about two people who were punished for doing wrong.

(Tune: "Where Is Thumbkin?")

Ananias and Sapphira                    (*Hold up one finger on each hand.*)
Told a lie, told a lie,
To the Holy Spirit, to the Holy Spirit.
Then they dropped dead.
Then they dropped dead.

All the people, all the people,          (*Hold up all fingers on each hand.*)
Brought their gifts, brought their gifts,
To help other people, to help other people.
God was pleased. God was pleased.

We can serve Him. We can serve Him,      (*Point up using one finger on each hand.*)
Every day, every day.
We can love and serve Him. We can love and serve Him.
We love God. We love God.

# God Made All

**Genesis 1**

Let the children perform this action rhyme to celebrate God's wonderful creation!

Butterfly, butterfly,
Flittering around the sky.
Butterfly, butterfly,
I love to watch you fly.

*(Cross arms and flutter hands.)*

Buzzy bee, buzzy bee,
Buzzing around the honey tree.
Buzzy bee, buzzy bee,
I hope you won't sting me.

*(Flitter fingers.)*

Hoppy toad, hoppy toad,
Taking leaps along the road.
Hoppy toad, hoppy toad,
You are a creature made by God.

*(Hop.)*

God made all, God made all
Creatures, creatures, big and small.
All God made was good, you see.
All God made was good, even me!

*(Sweep hands around to indicate "all.")*

*(Point to self.)*

# Mary and Martha

**Luke 10:38–42**

Children love the tune "Bingo" and will learn all about two of Jesus' special friends as they sing the song below. After the children learn this song, you can use some variations. You may sing one verse at a time, and then sing it faster and faster. Or, you may begin to leave out one word, then two, then three, then four, and finally all five (or six) syllables of the repeating line in each verse.

(Tune: "Bingo")

Mary and Martha had a good friend,
And Jesus was His name-o.
Jesus was His name.
Jesus was His name.
Jesus was His name.
And He came for a visit.

Martha wanted Mary to do some work,
But Mary just wanted to listen-o.
Mary wanted to learn.
Mary wanted to learn.
Mary wanted to learn,
From Jesus Christ our Lord.

Jesus said Mary was so right—
We should want to learn about God-o.
We should want to learn.
We should want to learn.
We should want to learn,
About our Holy God.

Example of how to leave out words/syllables from the first verse:

Jesus was His _____, Jesus was His _____, (*Clap hands for each blank.*)

Jesus was His _____. And He came for a visit.

Jesus was _____ _____, Jesus was _____ _____,

Jesus was _____ _____. And He came for a visit.

# Still

### Joshua 10:1–15; Matthew 8:23–26; Psalm 46:10

Use these chants for wiggle activities or to reinforce the Bible stories listed above. Teach the children the chants. Then tell the children to march in a circle. When you all say the word "still," everybody stops.

## Joshua 10:1–15

The sun stood **still**.
The sun stood **still**.
Till Joshua's army won the battle,
The sun stood **still**.

## Matthew 8:23–26

The storm became **still**.
The storm became **still**.
Jesus said, "Stop," and then
The storm became **still**.

## Psalm 46:10

*"Be **still**, and know that I am God . . ."*
*"Be **still**, and know that I am God . . ."*
 Psalm 46:10 says,
*"Be **still**, and know that I am God . . ."*

© Shining Star Publications

40

SS48842

# Picture Bingo

This game is perfect to use to reinforce such stories as Creation or Noah's Ark. Make enough copies of pages 42 and 43 so that each child will have one of the bingo cards. Cut out the cards. Cut out the picture squares below. Place the squares facedown. Choose one at a time, calling out the picture. The children then cover this picture on their cards. (Children can use cereal pieces, buttons, or paper scraps to cover the pictures.) To win, a child must have three squares filled in either vertically, horizontally, or diagonally.

© Shining Star Publications

SS48842

# Picture Bingo

continued

# Picture Bingo

### continued

© Shining Star Publications

SS48842

# Be Good!

These award circles make being good fun for children!

Make a copy of this page for each child. Cut out the circles. Keep a roll of tape handy. During class time, give children several opportunities to earn the award circles below.

I'm a good listener!

I'm a good helper!

I'm a good friend!

I'm a good Bible learner!

I'm a good singer!

I'm a good student!

When a child has earned one of the circles, tape it to his or her clothing. At the end of class, each child should have the six circles taped on him or her as a reward for being "good" in class. Make a big deal out of receiving the "good" awards. Learning will then become a fun game for the children.

© Shining Star Publications

SS48842

# The Resurrection

### Luke 19–24

The resurrection of Christ is such an important event for Christians! Let the children create the puzzle below to learn all about it.

Make a copy and cut out the puzzle as one whole piece for each child. Trace around the outside edge of the puzzle on construction paper to make a frame pattern for each puzzle. Cut out a frame for each child.

Let the children color and cut out the puzzle pieces and lay them aside. Discuss each symbol with the children. Then have the children place the pieces in the puzzle frame. They should begin with the pieces that form the cross.

© Shining Star Publications

SS48842

# A Story Wheel

## Luke 15:11–32

The Parable of the Lost Son is a favorite of many children. Review it with them. Then cut out the story wheel below. Tape it to the bottom of a paper plate. Spin the plate and have a child drop a paper clip onto the wheel. The child should then tell about the picture that the paper clip landed on.

© Shining Star Publications

SS48842

# Arm Tangle Time

This game is perfect to use with any story involving the pictures on the circles below and on page 48. Discuss each picture with the children before you begin.

Make two copies of the circles below and on page 48 and cut them out. Glue one set of circles in random order on a large sheet of construction paper to make a game board.

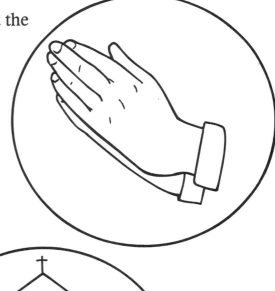

Place the second set of circles facedown. Place the game board in the center of a table where all children can reach it. If a table is not convenient to all children, then place the board on the floor and have the children sit around it. (If you have a large class, prepare one game for each group of 6–8 children.)

Choose a circle from the facedown (calling) pile. Call out the picture. The first child places a finger on the corresponding picture on the game board. Choose another picture for the next child. That child places his or her finger on the corresponding picture on the game board.

Children do not move their fingers away from their places on the board, but reach over others to touch their pictures. Play the game until all children have one or both arms entangled with the others. Explain to the children that all people must work together to love and serve God.

© Shining Star Publications

SS48842

# Arm Tangle Time

### continued

© Shining Star Publications

SS48842

# What's Missing?

## Genesis 44

Review the story of Joseph and the silver cup with the children. Then cut out the picture squares below and on page 50. Place them on a table or tape them to the wall. Have the children close their eyes. Remove one of the pictures. Let the children open their eyes and try to guess which picture is missing.

# What's Missing?

continued

# Jesus' Special Cousin

**Luke 1**

John the Baptist played an important role in Jesus' life. Help the children learn about him with the puppets below and on page 52.

Make enough copies of this page and page 52 so that each child gets one puppet. Cut out the puppets and let the children color them. Tape a craft stick to the back of each puppet. Tell each child which puppet he or she is holding.

Instruct the children to listen carefully while you tell the story of the birth of John the Baptist. When you mention the puppets the children are holding, the children should hold up their puppets.

For more fun, make a set of puppets for each child and allow time for children to role-play the story. Or, the puppets may be used as a mobile craft for children to make and take home.

angel

friends

© Shining Star Publications

SS48842

# Jesus' Special Cousin

**continued**

Elizabeth

priests

Zechariah

baby John

© Shining Star Publications

SS48842

# Fill-the-Page Bingo

### Luke 1–2

This game is the perfect way to remind children of our Lord's birth. Make enough copies of this page and page 54 so that each child has one card. Use unpopped corn or dried beans for markers. Make two copies of the picture cards. Cut apart one set to use for calling cards. Place called-out cards on the uncut copy.

A child wins when his or her entire card is covered. This game will familiarize the children with the people and objects in the Christmas story.

For more fun, stop the game a few times. Ask for volunteers to tell what each of the pictures means in the Christmas story.

## Picture Cards

## Card 1                    Card 2

# Fill-the-Page Bingo

continued

**Card 3**
**Card 4**

**Card 5**
**Card 6**

© Shining Star Publications

SS48842

# Hide-and-Seek Bingo

### Galatians 5:22–23

Everyone needs to pray for the fruit of the Spirit. Teach the children all about this concept with this game.

Divide the children into two or more teams. Make two copies of the bingo cards below for each team. Glue each team's two bingo cards to construction paper (the same color). Each team gets a different color. (For example, Team A's two bingo cards could be glued on red paper.)

Give each team one copy of its bingo card. Cut the other bingo card apart and hide the pieces. Teams search for all of the pieces to match their color of card and place the pieces on it.

# Listen Closely!

**Numbers 22:21–41; Luke 19:28–38**

These ears are fun for the children to wear as they hear stories involving donkeys.

Make a copy of this page for each child. Have the children color and cut out the donkey ears. The children can put on their donkey ears (hold up to their own ears) whenever they hear the word *donkey*.

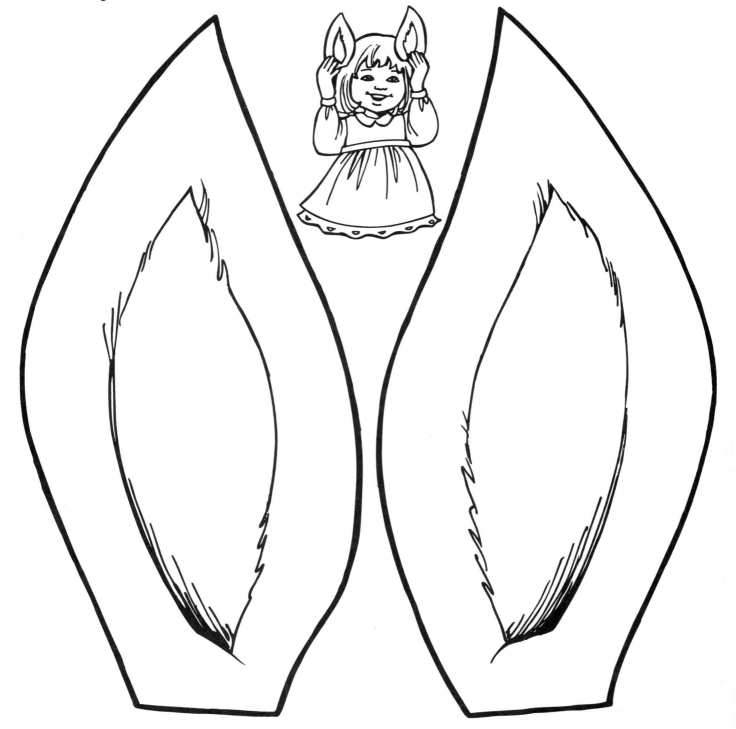

# A Super Star

This is a perfect way to build children's self-esteem!

Make copies of this page so that you will have several stars for each child. Cut out the stars. During a lesson or story, stop several times and ask a question. The child who knows the answer gets a star. The child with the most stars at the end of the lesson wins a reward.

© Shining Star Publications

SS48842

# 10 Terrible Plagues

**Exodus 7–11**

Tell the children the story of the ten plagues so that they understand the pictures on the cards below and on page 59. Stress that the plagues happened to the Egyptians, who were enemies of God's people. Then help the children glue two copies of this page and page 59 to construction paper. The children may color and cut apart the cards.

To play the game, place cards facedown. Player one chooses two cards. If they match, the child keeps the pair. If they don't match, both cards are put back facedown.

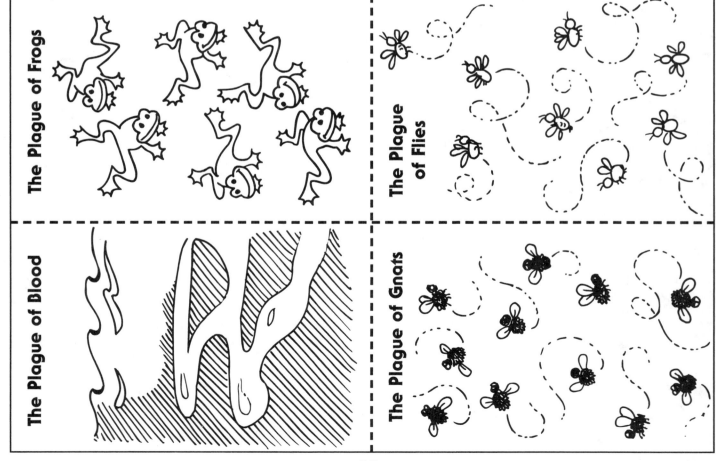

The Plague of Frogs

The Plague of Flies

The Plague of Blood

The Plague of Gnats

The Plague on Livestock

The Plague of Boils

The Plague of Hail

The Plague of Locusts

The Plague of Darkness

The Plague on the Firstborn Son

# Noah Dominoes

**Genesis 6–9**

The story of Noah's Ark is a favorite of all children. Let the children have fun with this story as they play the game below.

Make a copy of this page and pages 61–62 for each child or for the group. Glue the pages to construction paper. (You may also want to make a classroom set on sturdy cardboard.)

Children may color and cut out the dominoes. To start the game, turn all dominoes facedown except for one. Each player chooses one domino on each turn. A domino may be placed in the playing area if it matches a domino not played on yet (the matching ends are placed together). Double pictures (two of the same on a domino) should be placed sideways, providing another direction for the game to go.

# Noah Dominoes

continued

© Shining Star Publications

SS48842

# Noah Dominoes

continued

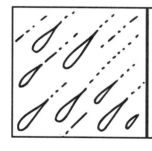 

© Shining Star Publications

SS48842

# A Special Man

**Exodus 19–20**

Review the story of Moses, Mt. Sinai, and the Ten Commandments with the children. Then make two copies of this page for each child or group. You may want to glue the pages to construction paper to make them more sturdy.

After the children color and cut out the boxes, help them fold them and tape them together. Children can use dried beans as markers. A child throws the boxes onto the table. If the child gets a pair, he or she gets a marker to keep until the end of the game. The one with the most markers at the end wins.

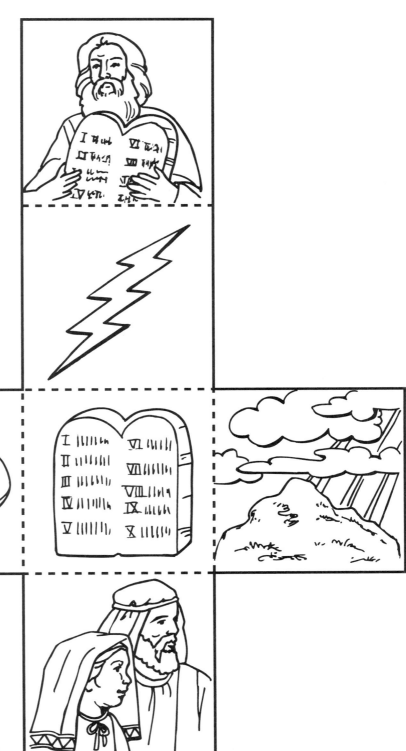

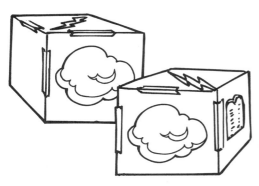

# Paul's Journeys

## Acts 9–28

Acquaint the children with some of Paul's adventures by playing this game in class. Use squares of colorful paper as playing pieces for the game board below and on page 65. Assemble the cube below. Children roll the cube to determine how far to move.

Miss a turn.

4

3   1   2

Take an extra turn.

Start

Move 3 spaces across the sea.

• Rome

Finish!

Shipwreck! Go back 1 space.

PAUL'S JOURNE

© Shining Star Publications

SS48842

# Paul's Journeys

**continued**

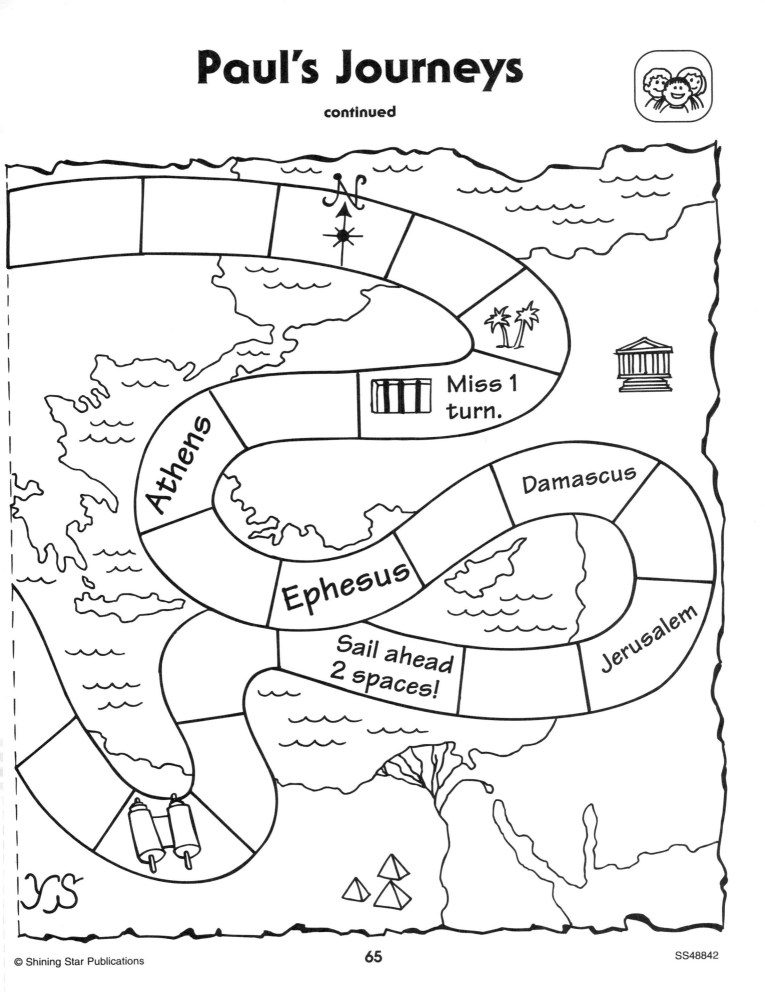

© Shining Star Publications

SS48842

# Tic-Tac-Toe

**Matthew 25:31–46**

This game is great to play to reinforce the story of "The Sheep and the Goats."

Make a copy of this page for each child. Have the children color the sheep and goats and cut them out. They should also cut out the tic-tac-toe board. Children may play the game with a friend or take it home to play.

# Race to Give

## Luke 21:1–4

Explain to the children that God wants us to give to the church to help others in need. Tell them that people have been giving to the church since Bible times. Then let them play this game. You may want to share the story of "The Widow's Offering" (Luke 21:1–4).

Two children at a time can play this game. Cut out and tape together the two strips below to make one long game board. Have the pair of children take turns tossing a coin. If it lands on heads, they move 1 space; if tails, they move 2 spaces. The children can use pebbles, paper circles, two different kinds of coins, or any items that fit inside the squares for playing pieces. The first child to get to the treasure chest wins. This is a no-reading game, so children can play with a minimum amount of supervision.

**Strip 2**

**Strip 1**

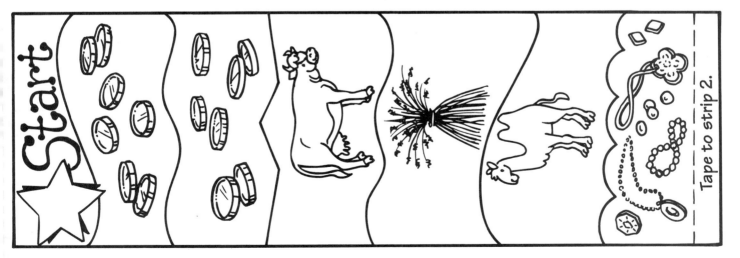

# Catch a Coin

**Matthew 17:24–27**

This card game is a fun way for the children to learn all about the story of "The Temple Tax." Make a copy of this page and pages 69–70. Color the pages and glue them to construction paper. Then cut out the cards. This game is for 2–4 children. To play the game, the cards are dealt out until all are used. The children lay down any matching sets of three cards that they are holding. Then the first player begins by picking one card from any player. The next child does the same thing, picking a card from a child of his or her choice. Any time a child gets three matching cards, the child should lay them down in front of him or her. At the end of the game, one child will be left holding the coin card.

# Catch a Coin

continued

# Catch a Coin

continued

# Climbing Jacob's Ladder

**Genesis 28:10–22**

Children will have a lot of fun learning about "Jacob's Dream at Bethel" with this game.

This game can be played by 2–4 children. Have children color and cut out the game board, the cards, and the playing pieces (people) below and on page 72. The people pieces can be folded and taped in half so that they stand up.

To play the game, place the cards facedown. Children take turns drawing a card and moving the number of spaces written on it. Children move up the ladder to heaven.

Tape.

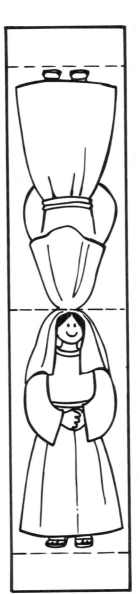

© Shining Star Publications

SS48842

# Climbing Jacob's Ladder

continued

© Shining Star Publications

72

SS48842

# Coat of Many Colors

**Genesis 37:1–4**

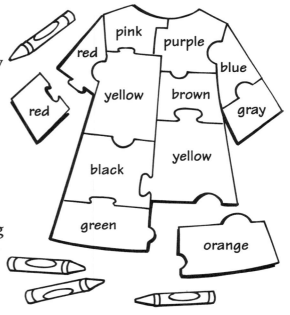

Children can make their own coats of many colors and learn all about the story as they play this game.

This game can be played with 2–4 children. Make a copy of the coat on page 74 for each child. Have the children cut out their coat puzzles and write a color (using only those included below) on each puzzle piece. They may use a color twice. Then color the squares below the appropriate colors and cut them out.

Put the color squares in a stack facedown. A child picks up a square and says the color. He or she colors the appropriate puzzle piece on his or her coat, thus coloring the coat as he or she plays. Only the child who drew the color gets to color. Then the next child takes a turn. The object of the game is to be the first one to complete the coat of many colors.

| pink | red | orange | yellow | green |
|------|------|--------|--------|-------|
| blue | black | brown | purple | gray |
| pink | red | orange | yellow | green |
| blue | black | brown | purple | gray |
| pink | red | orange | yellow | green |
| blue | black | brown | purple | gray |

© Shining Star Publications

SS48842

# Coat of Many Colors

continued

© Shining Star Publications

74

SS48842

# Follow the Star

**Matthew 2:1–12**

This game is fun for children and helps them learn how the wise men found baby Jesus.

To make a spinner, cut a 1/2" x 2" strip of construction paper and loosely fasten it to the dot in the middle of the star with a paper fastener. To make playing pieces, cut a 1" x 3" strip in a different color for each child. Fold these pieces in half to make them stand.

Children take turns spinning the spinner and moving the number of spaces indicated on it. The first one to baby Jesus wins.

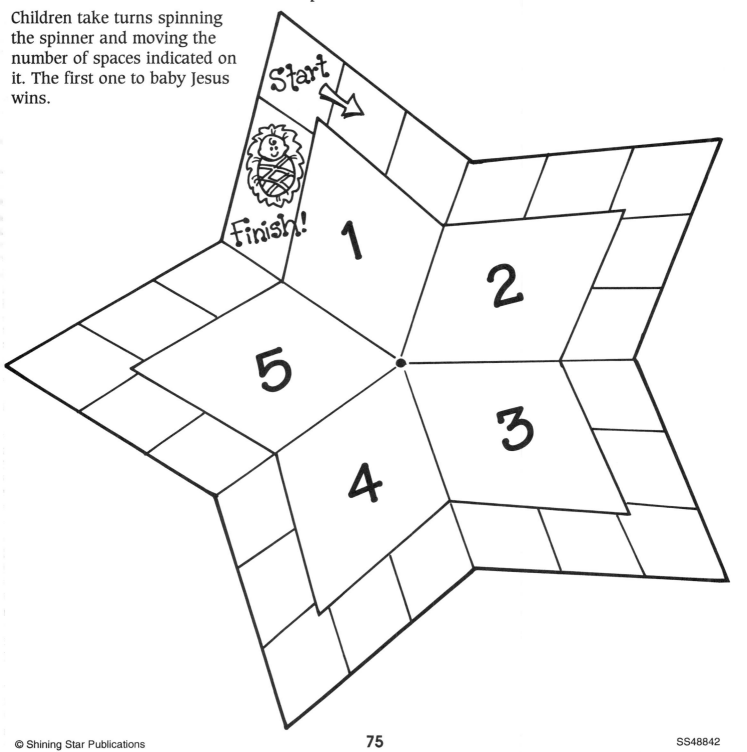

© Shining Star Publications

SS48842

# No-Read Miracles Fun

Discuss the many ways Jesus cured the sick and dying with the children. Then let them play this game to reinforce Jesus' healing powers. Be sure to discuss the symbols on the game board (pages 77 and 78) with the children (sunglasses—healing blind people; crutch—healing lame people; ear—healing deaf people; bandages—bringing dead people back to life; empty mat—healing the very sick).

Make a copy of this page and pages 77–78. Cut out the die and color it the indicated colors. Use these same four colors to color the correct spaces on the game board. This makes a no-read game. Fold the die into a cube and tape the edges. For game pieces, use coins or dried beans.

Children take turns rolling the die and moving to the nearest square of that color. If they land on a happy face, they move one space and then get another turn. If they land on a sad face, they miss their turn.

Miss a turn.

red

Take another turn.

blue

yellow

green

# No-Read Miracles Fun

continued

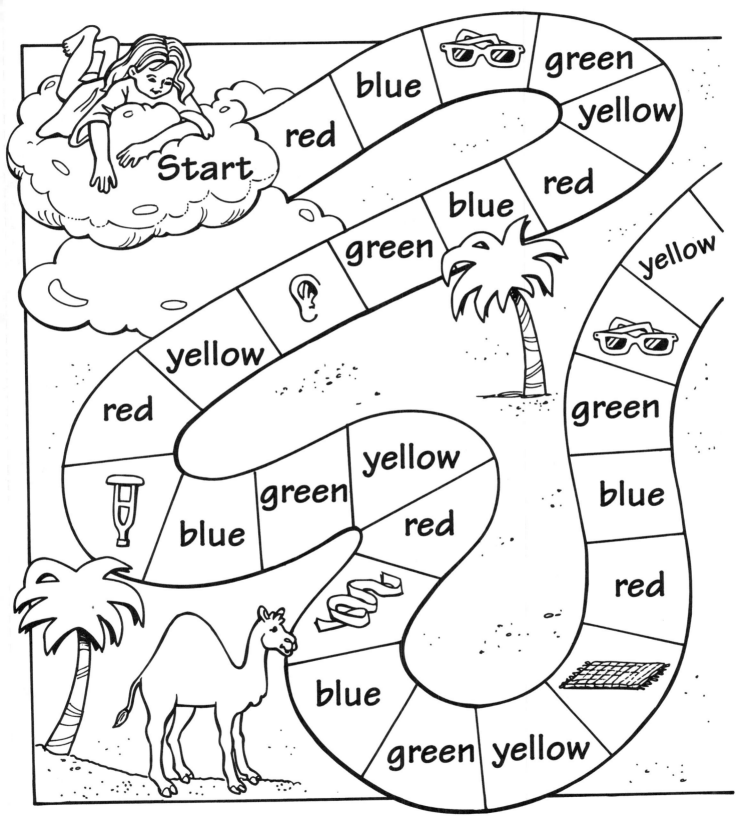

# No-Read Miracles Fun

**continued**

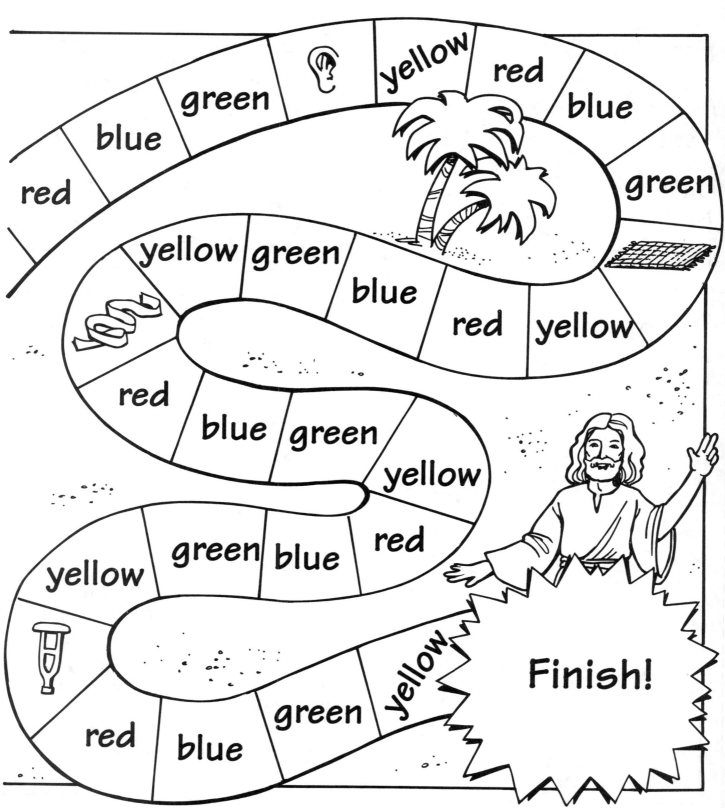

red
blue
green
yellow
red
blue
green
yellow
green
blue
red
yellow
red
blue
green
yellow
red
yellow
green
blue
red
yellow
red
blue
green
yellow
Finish!

# Growing in the Garden

### Genesis 2

This game provides children with a fun way to learn about Adam and Eve and the Garden of Eden.

Make a copy of this page and page 80 for each child. Have the children color and cut out the tree, the squares with the fruit, and the die. Help the children fold and tape their dice. Divide the children into pairs and have each child place the tree in front of him or her and spread out the fruit pieces.

To play, the pairs of children take turns rolling their dice to find out what fruit to place on their trees. If a child rolls the serpent, he or she removes all of his or her fruit and starts over. The first child to get all of his or her fruit on the tree wins.

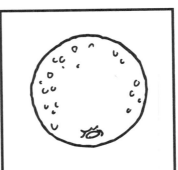

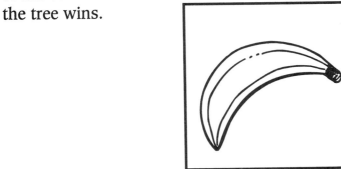

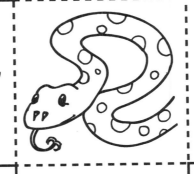

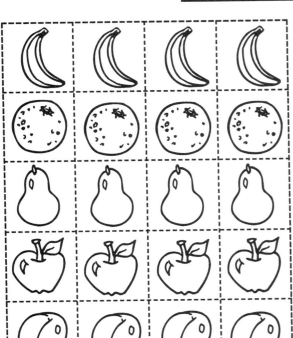

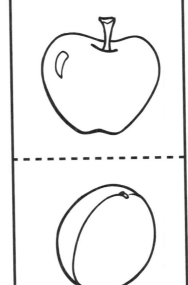

© Shining Star Publications

SS48842

# Growing in the Garden

### continued

© Shining Star Publications

80

SS48842

# A Very Special Baby

**Luke 2**

This game reminds the children of the miraculous birth of baby Jesus. To review the story, use the cards before the game as flashcards. Ask the children how each picture relates to the story of Jesus' birth.

Make a copy of this page and page 82. Color and cut out all the cards. To play the game, place the cards facedown on a table in an array. The first child chooses two cards. If they match, he or she gets to keep them. If they do not match, they must be turned over. Remember, the pictures on the cards must match *exactly*. The child with most pairs at the end of the game wins.

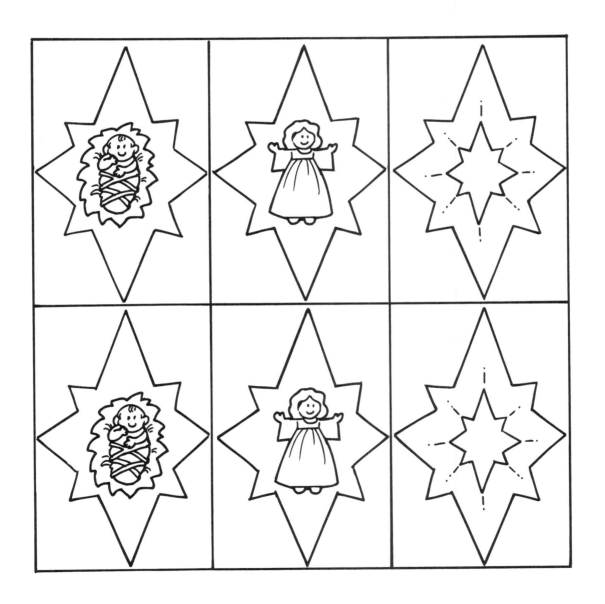

© Shining Star Publications

SS48842

# A Very Special Baby

continued

© Shining Star Publications

82

SS48842

# Fish in the Net

**Luke 5:1–11**

Review the story of "The Calling of the First Disciples" with the children. Then let them play the puzzle game below.

Make one copy of this page for each child. Then glue each page to construction paper and cut out the net shapes. Children can color and cut out the fish shapes.

On "go," children race to fit their fish together in the net.

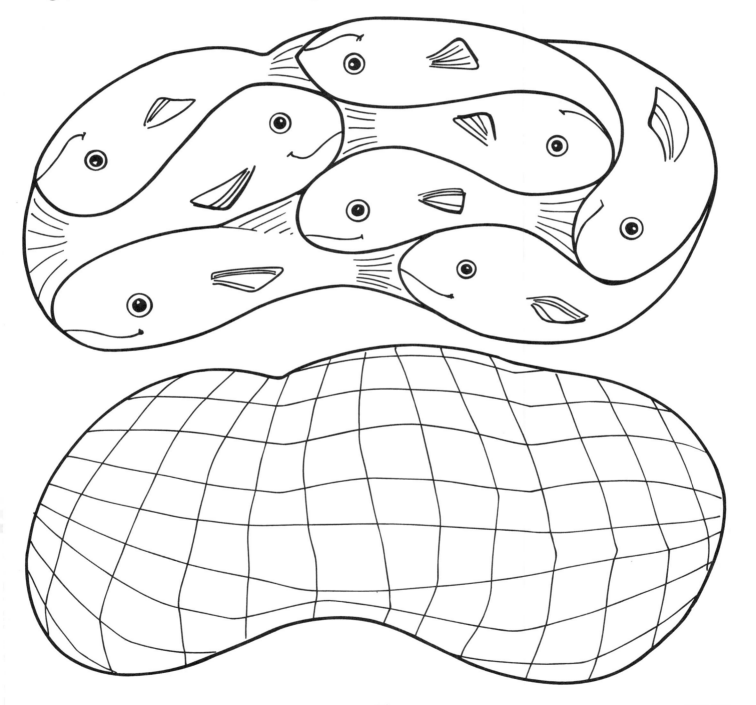

© Shining Star Publications

SS48842

# Wind and Flames

## Acts 2:2–4

The children will learn all about the Holy Spirit as they play this game.

Make a copy of this page for each child. Give each child a straw. Let the children color and cut out their flames.

To play, have each child pick up one of his or her flames by sucking in using the straw. The children will walk to a designated area and put each flame down.

For more fun, have the children sit in pairs across a table from one another. The children can blow a flame back and forth to demonstrate a mighty wind.

© Shining Star Publications

SS48842

# Joseph's Dreams

## Genesis 41:1–40

Children will have fun learning about Pharaoh's dreams and Joseph's interpretation of them as they play this game.

Make one copy of this page and page 86 per group of 2–4 children. Cut out the cards. Cut out the cube, fold it, and tape it together.

To play, divide the wheat cards equally among the 2–4 children. If there is an uneven number of wheat cards, lay the extra cards aside. Each child takes a turn rolling the cube onto the table or floor. If a child gets bowing wheat, he or she collects one wheat card from each of the other players. If the child gets the angry brothers, he or she gives each player a wheat card. Otherwise, the next child takes a turn. Game ends when one child has all the wheat cards.

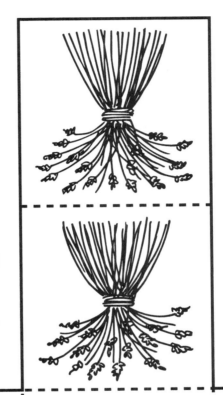

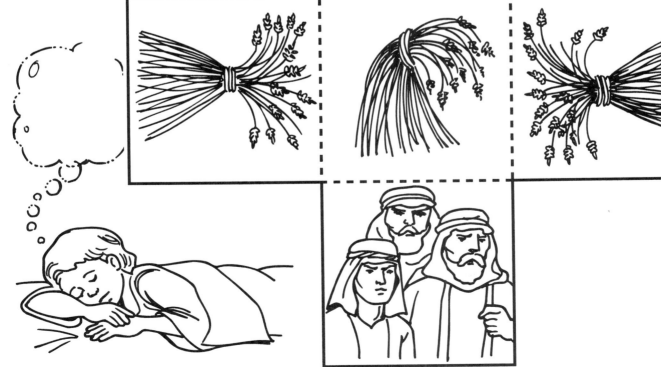

© Shining Star Publications

SS48842

# Joseph's Dreams
### continued

© Shining Star Publications

SS48842

# Racing Camels

This game is perfect to use with any Bible story involving animals or travel.

Give a copy of this page, one toilet paper tube, and a length of string about six feet long to each pair of children. Help the children fold their camels in half and tape the toilet paper tube inside this fold toward the top. (See illustration.)

To play, each pair of children will stretch out a piece of yarn or string between them. Help them place one end of their yarn or string through the tissue tube. Show them how to keep the yarn or string tight and raise or lower one end to make the camel move.

After the children have mastered the technique of moving the camels, have some races for fun.

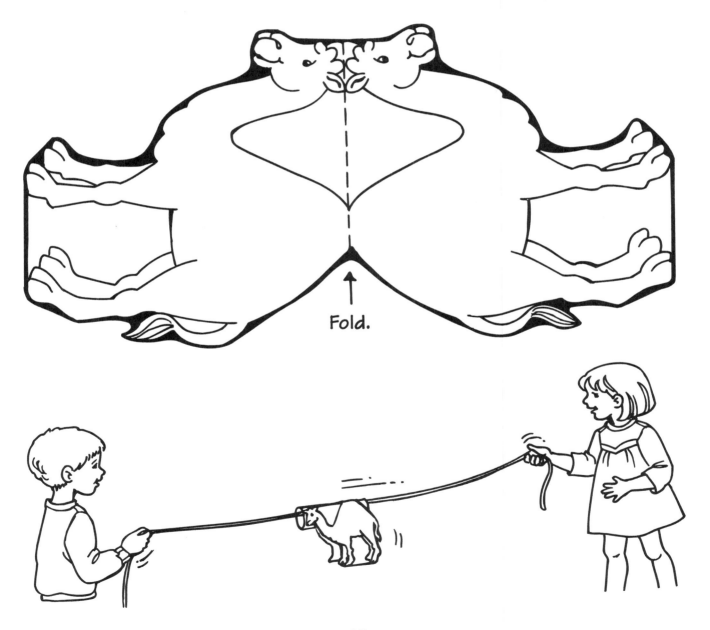

Fold.

© Shining Star Publications SS48842

# Wandering Around

### Exodus and Deuteronomy

The children can pretend to wander in the wilderness like the Israelites did for 40 years as they play this game.

Make a copy of this page and page 89 for every pair of children. Help the children cut out and construct the dice. For playing pieces, use a penny and a nickel (or any small items that will fit inside the squares). The object of the game is to reach a goal while following directions. This is a no-read game.

To play, a child rolls both dice. One die tells the children in which direction to go, and the other die tells them how many squares to move. If the child does not have room to move all the spaces indicated on the dice in one row, he or she may not drop down to another row until the child rolls a "down."

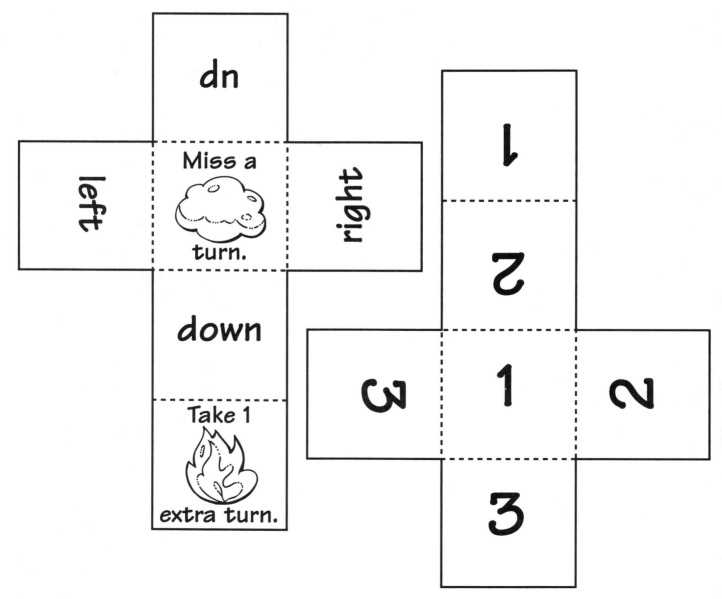

# Wandering Around

**continued**

▼

FINISH

89

# Famous People Boxes

These boxes are a great way for children to learn about famous people in the Bible.

Make a copy of this page and page 91 for each child. After the children color the pages, help them cut out the patterns, fold, and tape them to form boxes. Before closing the last flap, let the children add a few dried beans or some rice inside.

Let the children play with the boxes. As they toss and catch one of the boxes, have them tell about one of the famous people.

# Famous People Boxes

continued

# Catch Me If You Can!

### Jonah 1–4

This game is fun for the children to play and will remind them of the large fish that swallowed Jonah.

## Materials Needed:

one copy of this page and a juice can or large paper cup for each child

crayons

scissors

tape

string

large paper clip for weight

## Directions:

Have the children color the pictures. Then help them cut out the patterns. Tape the large fish pattern around the can or cup. Tape a length of string to the bottom of the can or cup.

Fold the pattern of Jonah in half. Place the paper clip inside and then tape the sides together. Tape the loose end of the string onto Jonah's feet.

The object of the game is to flip Jonah up and try to catch him inside the "fish."

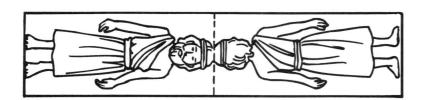

# Where Do They Live?

Give each child a copy of this page. Help the children decide which creature lives in each home. They should draw a line from each creature to its home and color the pictures. Discuss God's care of each of His creatures.

# Find Matching Fish

This activity is perfect to use with any story involving Creation, Noah, fishermen, or fish. Give each child a copy of this page. Help the children color like pairs of fish.

© Shining Star Publications

# Wise and Foolish Builders

**Matthew 7:24–27**

Give each child a copy of this page. As the children work to find nine things in the picture that they might use to build a house, discuss the story of "The Wise and Foolish Builders" with them.

© Shining Star Publications

SS48842

# Silly Scenes

**Genesis 1:1–27**

This is a fun way to help children learn all about God's wonderful creation.

Give each child a copy of this page. Have the children color the pictures. Then help them cut out the cards and cut each one in half on the dotted lines. Encourage the children to make silly figures by putting different tops and bottoms together.

© Shining Star Publications

SS48842